NIGHT-SKY CHECKER BOARD

Phoneme Media
1551 Colorado Blvd., Suite 201
Los Angeles, California 90041

First Edition, 2016

Originally published in Korean in 2011

Night-Sky Checkerboard is published under the
support of Literature Translation Institute of Korea (LTI Korea).

ISBN: 978-1-939419-47-7

Library of Congress Control Number: 2015945799

Cover art by Maggie Chiang

Cover Design by Jaya Nicely

Typesetting by Scott Arany

This book is distributed by Publishers Group West

Printed in the United States of America

Phoneme Media is a nonprofit publishing and film production house, a
fiscally sponsored project of Pen Center USA, dedicated to disseminating
and promoting literature in translation through books and film.

Curious books for curious people

NIGHT-SKY CHECKER BOARD

POEMS BY
OH SAE-YOUNG

TRANSLATED FROM THE KOREAN
BY BROTHER ANTHONY OF TAIZÉ

PHONEME
MEDIA
Los Angeles

CONTENTS

NIGHT-SKY CHECKERBOARD (2011)

EARLIER POEMS

OH SAE-YOUNG
오세영

Oh Sae-young was born in Yongkwang, South Jeolla Province, in 1942. He studied at the Korean Language and Literature Department of Seoul National University, where he later taught for many years as a professor. He is now an Emeritus Professor there. He began his literary career in April 1965, when his first poems were published in the review *Hyeondae Munhak*. He has published some twelve volumes of poetry as well as a number of volumes of literary essays. He has received several awards for his work.

He was initially fascinated by Modernism, and attempted to represent the inner landscapes of the dislocated self produced by industrial society. From there, he gradually moved in the direction of a quest for an ontological authenticity in life. Later, he attempted to explore the existential meaning of things by means of Eastern modes of thought. His poetry as a whole is characterized by the pursuit of a harmonious fusion of the lyrical with the ideological, and the desire to give new formal expression to tradition by the techniques of Modernism.

The present volume contains all the poems published in 2011 in the volume *Night-Sky Checkerboard* and a small number of earlier poems.

—Brother Anthony of Taizé

I

밤 하늘의
바둑판

NIGHT-SKY CHECKER BOARD

(2011)

눈 발자국

누가 시킨 운필인가.
나 한 개 꿈꾸는 볼펜이 되어 눈밭에
또박또박
서정시 한 행을 써 내려 간다.

미루나무 가지 끝에 앉아 졸고 있다가
문득
설해목(雪害木) 부러지는 소리에 눈을 뜬
까치 한 마리,
까악까악
낭랑한 목소리로 읊고 있다.
그 시 한 구절.

Footsteps in Snow

Who asked me to write this?
Turning into a dreaming ballpoint, on the snowy ground
neatly
I inscribe one lyric line, then make my way down.

A magpie,
dozing perched at the tip of a poplar branch,
abruptly
opens its eyes at the sound of a snow-laden branch breaking.
Caw-caw,
it is reciting in a resonant voice—
one passage from that poem.

팽이

문밖
매섭게 겨울바람 쏠리는 소리,
휘이익
내리치는 채찍에
온 산이 운다.

누가 지구를
팽이 치는 것일까.
봄, 여름, 가을 그리고 드디어 겨울,
회전이 느슨해질 때마다 사정 없이
옷싹
서릿발 갈기는 그 회초리,
강추위로 부는 바람.

하늘은 항상
미끄러운 빙판길이다.

A Top

Out of doors,
the sound of a bitter winter wind slashing past.
Crack,
under the whip's blows
the whole mountain weeps.

Who can be whipping the globe
like a top?
Spring, summer, autumn, and winter too,
whenever its turning slackens, mercilessly,
appalling,
that sharply lashing cane,
a bitterly cold wind blows.

The sky is always
a slippery, icy path.

강설(降雪)

산간 오두막집,
굴뚝으로 한줄기 연기를 피워 올리자
지체 없이 투입되는 병력.
하늘엔 일사 분란하게 하강하는 낙하산들로 온통
가득 찼다.
지상에 내린 하얀 스키복의 공수대원들에게
재빨리 접수되는 겨울 산.
이곳저곳 간단없이 출몰하던
멧돼지, 고라니들이 자취를 감췄다.
한 순간에 제압된
숲속 게릴라들의 준동.

Snow Falling

A hillside hut.
As soon as a trail of smoke rose from the chimney
armed men were sent in without delay.
The sky was full
of parachutes descending in perfect order.
The winter mountains quickly welcomed
the paratroopers as they landed in their white ski wear.
The wild boars and deer, frequently seen here and there,
concealed their tracks.
Maneuvers of forest guerillas,
mastered in a flash.

피항(避港)

명절날
거실에 모여 즐겁게 다과(茶菓)를 드는
온 가족의 단란한 웃음소리,
가즈런히 놓인 현관의 빈 신발들이
코를 마주대한 채
쫑긋
귀를 열고 있다.

내항(內港)의 부두에
일렬로 정연히 밧줄에 묶여
일제히 뭍을 돌아다보고 서 있는 빈 선박들의
용골.
잠시 먼 바다의 파랑을 피하는 그
잔잔한 흔들림.

Harbor

On a holiday,
harmonious laughter echoes as the whole family
takes tea together gathered in the living room,
while the empty shoes lying evenly spaced in the vestibule,
their noses turned toward one another,
prick up their ears and listen attentively.

Along the wharfs of the inner harbor,
tied up neatly side by side
the keels
of empty ships standing together gazing shoreward,
briefly escaping the distant ocean's waves,
rock gently.

간첩

겨울 숲.
비트에 몸을 숨긴 딱따구리 한 마리
예의(銳意)
주위를 경계하며 다다 따따따 다다
난수표에 따라
비밀 암호를 타전한다.
"거점 확보, 오바"
산 너머 대기 중인 봄이
예하 부대에 긴급히 내리는 명령,

진군이다.
행동개시!

A Spy

Winter woodland.
A woodpecker, body hidden in the beat,
intently
surveying the surroundings, *ta-ta tatata ta-ta*,
sends a secret coded message
following the table of random digits.
"Secure base, over."
Lying in wait beyond the hills, spring
urgently transmits the order to its subordinate forces.

Time to advance.
Deploy!

나침반

　‘?’　표를 하고
호수의 오리 가족 한 떼 분주히 발을 놀려
수면 위를 헤엄친다.
한 놈, 두 놈 차례로 자맥질도 한다.
무엇을 찾고 있을까.
어제
밤하늘을 날다가 실수로 떨어뜨린
그 나침반인지도 몰라.

A Compass

Shaped like question marks,
on the lake a family of ducks is busily moving its legs
as they swim across the surface.
One or two at a time they dive beneath the water.
What are they looking for?
Perhaps it's the compass they carelessly dropped
yesterday
as they were flying through the night sky.

비행운(飛行雲)

한낮
뇌우(雷雨)를 동반한 천둥번개로
하늘 한 모서리가 조금
찢어진 모양,
대기 중 산소가 샐라
제트기 한 대가 긴급발진
천을 덧 대 바늘로 정교히
박음질 한다.

노을에 비껴
하얀 실밥이 더 선명해 보이는
한줄기 긴
비행운(飛行雲).

Vapor Trail

The thunder and lightning accompanying the thunderstorm
at midday
seem to have torn one edge of the sky,
the oxygen in the air is leaking away.
A jet plane
scrambles, comes flying fast
and carefully mends the cloth
with rapid lockstitch.

As it heads into the twilight,
the white seam is clearly visible—
a long
vapor trail.

정좌(正坐)

얼음 풀려
강물은 들녘에 일필휘지
문장을 갈겨쓰는데
온 종일
흐르는 물에 비친 제 모습을 들여다 보는
바위의 묵언(黙言),
글은 곧 사람일지니
한자 한자
정성들여 운필하는 지면의 저
새하얀 한지가
바람에 불려 날아가지 않도록
그 한 귀퉁이를 눌러 조붓이
앉아 있는
문진(文鎭)이여.

Sitting Straight

Freed of ice,
the river scrawls a sentence
across the fields, a single brush-stroke,
the silence of the rock,
that has spent the whole day
gazing at its reflection in the flowing water,
fears the writing might soon disappear
so to keep the white page,
on which the writing is being carefully inscribed
word by word,
from being blown away by the wind
it presses down on one corner,
a tightly squeezed
paperweight.

구름

구름은
하늘 유리창을 닦는 걸레,
쥐어짜면 주르르
물이 흐른다.

입김으로 훅 불어
지우고 보고, 지우고
다시 들여다보는 늙은 신의
호기심어린 눈빛.

The Cloud

The cloud
is a cloth rubbing at heaven's windows.
If you squeeze it,
water runs out.

Breathing, *puff*,
then rubbing, rubbing away
before peeping out again, old God's
prying eyes.

마사히 마라

하늘 유리창을 통해 들여다보는
저 무수히 깜박이는 눈,
눈동자들.
지구는 우주의
거대한 사파리일지도 몰라.

어떤 문제를 일으켰을까.
오늘도
유성(流星)의 총탄에 맞아 실신한
여린 영혼 하나,
마취뙌 채
지구 밖으로 끄을려 나간다.
저항할 틈도 없이……

Masai Mara

Those countless twinkling eyes
peeping down through heaven's windows.
Those eyes . . .
The world seems to be the universe's
great safari.

Has it been causing trouble?
One tender soul,
out cold after being struck by a meteor bullet,
still anesthetized,
is drawn up from the earth,
no time to resist . . .

첫사랑

여름 한낮
무더위로 하얗게 굳어가는 햇빛 속에서
정적에 짓눌린 개구리 하나
첨벙,
연못으로 뛰어드는 물소리.

화들짝
나른한 오수(午睡)에서 깨어나 살포시
눈꺼풀을 치켜뜨고
먼 하늘 바라보는 수련(睡蓮)의 파란
눈빛.

FIRST LOVE

Summer high noon,
crushed by the silence as the sunlight
hardens white in the heat, one frog—
splash,
the sound as it jumps into the pond.

Startled,
waking out of a sluggish doze, feebly
lifting an eyelid
and gazing skyward, the blue gaze
of a water lily.

번개 (3)

어둠 속에서
와장창,
하늘을 깨고 뛰어든 자객의
번득이는 칼날.
태양을 넘보는 산정 (山頂)의
키 큰 노거수(老巨樹) 하나를 향해 날라든다.

털썩
자신의 용상에서 쓰러져 나뒹구는
천년왕국.

Lightning (3)

Out of the darkness,
crack,
smashing the heavens, hurtling down,
the assassin's gleaming blade
goes flying
toward one towering old mountaintop tree
rivalling the sun.

Crash,
toppled from its throne, sprawling,
a thousand-year reign ends.

일몰(日沒)

온 종일 지구를 끌다가
저물 녘
지평선에 누워 비로소
안식에 든 산맥.

하루의 노역을 마치고
평화롭게
짚 바닥에 쓰러져 홀로 되새김질하는
소잔등의
처연하게 부드러운 능선이여.

Sunset

Having drawn the globe all day long,
when dusk falls
reclining at last on the horizon,
resting, a mountain range.

The sadly gentle ridge-line
of an ox's back,
the day's labor now over,
reclining on a straw-strewn floor all alone chewing the cud
peacefully.

푸른 스커트의 지퍼

농부는
대지의 성감대가 어디 있는지를
잘 안다.
욕망에 들뜬 열을 가누지 못해
가쁜 숨을 몰아쉬기조차 힘든 어느 봄날,
농부는 과감하게 대지를 쓰러뜨리고
쟁기로
그녀의 푸른 스커트의 지퍼를 연다.
아, 눈부시게 드러나는
분홍빛 속살,
삽과 괭이의 그 음탕한 애무, 그리고
벌린 땅속으로 흘리는 몇 알의 씨앗.
대지는 잠시 전율한다.
맨몸으로 누워 있는 그녀 곁에서
일어나 땀을 닦는 농부의 그 황홀한 노동,
그는 이미
대지가 언제 출산의 기쁨을 갖을까를 안다.
그의 튼실한 남근이 또
언제 일어설지를 안다.

A Green Skirt's Zipper

The farmer
knows full well
where to find the ground's erogenous zones.
One spring day, unable to share the fever aroused by desire,
finding it hard even to breathe freely,
the farmer boldly overwhelms the ground
then, with his plow,
opens her green skirt's zipper.
Ah, dazzling, the exposed
pink flesh,
and after lascivious caresses with spade and hoe,
a few seeds flow into the gaping ground
as the earth trembles briefly.
As she lies there naked, beside her
the farmer's rapturous labor, as he wipes away his sweat.
He knows already
just when the ground will experience the joy of giving birth.
And he knows too just when his own sturdy penis
will stir and rise.

축제

해마다 일월이면
강원도(江原道) 인제(麟蹄) 땅 소양호(昭陽湖)에선
각지에서 몰려든 수만 인파로
살생을 낙(樂)을 삼아 흥청이나니
일컬어 빙어(氷魚)축제라 한다.
호수의 얼음을 깨고 혹은 꼬챙이로 찍어 혹은
바늘로 꿰어 잡아 올린 빙어를
한쪽에선 굽고,
한쪽에선 튀기고,
한쪽에선 끓이고
또 한쪽에서는 살아 팔딱 거리는 그대로
초장에 찍어 냉큼 목에 넘기면서
참 즐거운 하루였다고 무릎을 친다.
살을 태우는 그 연기여, 냄새여.
신(神)이 인간을 잡아 이토록 회를 쳐 먹어도
즐거운 손가.
나 비록 채식주의자는 아니고
불문(佛門)에 입교한 빈도(貧道)는 더더욱 아니건만
차마 이 아비규환(阿鼻叫喚)을 축제라
부를 수는 없구나.

A Festival

Every year in January,
at Soyang Lake in Inje, Gangwon Province,
large crowds gather from all over
and revel in the joys of slaughter,
calling it the Smelt Festival.
After smashing the ice on the lake, or hacking at it with a stick,
or
piercing it with a needle, the smelt they've caught
here they grill,
here they fry,
here they boil,
and here they swallow straight, dipped in sauce, alive and
twitching,
then slap their knees: What a happy day!
Smoke from burning flesh! Smell it!
If a god caught humans and ate them raw like this
would that be fun?
It's not that I'm a vegetarian,
let alone a devout Buddhist monk,
but I cannot call this hellish scene
a festival.

생명표 브랜드

고르게 공급하는 전력이 제대로
공장을 돌리는 것처럼
때 맞춰 대는 물이 또한
논밭을 잘 가동시킨다.
물로 만드느냐.
불로 만드느냐.
이 세상 모든 것은 공장의 제품,
자연은 물로 돌아가는 공장이다.
거미줄처럼 얽힌 저 물길들의
전선을 보아라.
지상의 강물은 고압선,
지하의 수맥들은 일반선,
농부는 오늘도 저수지에서
잘 변압된 전기를 끌어와
논밭을 가동시킨다.
질서 정연하게 돌아가는 생산라인의
하자 없는 제품,
그 생명표 브랜드.

Life Brand

Just as a regular supply of electricity
keeps a factory turning,
so a properly regulated supply of water
keeps the fields going.
Made by water?
Made by fire?
Everything in this world is factory producd,
nature being a factory driven by water.
Just consider that grid of waterways
tangled together like a spider's web.
Rivers above ground the high-tension network,
underground veins the local lines.
Today again the farmer draws
properly transformed current from the reservoir
to operate his fields.
Flawless products
off the smoothly running production line,
Life brand.

복토(覆土)

만성 위염으로
기운이 쇠잔하여 이제 드러눕게 된 몸,
영양제, 항생제로 겨우겨우 버티다가
할 수 없이
이 봄
외과 처방을 받는다.

지력(地力)이 다해 복토한 논을
오늘 처음으로 흙을 골라 골을 치고
써래질 한다.

위 절개 봉합 수술.

Field Work

Weakened by chronic gastritis,
the body lies prostrate,
barely sustained by tonics and antibiotics
and finally, no other choice,
with spring,
surgery is prescribed.

Its fertility restored, covered with fresh soil,
today leveling and spreading earth for the first time
the paddy field is harrowed.

Stiching up the incision in the stomach.

파업

앞 다투어 시커멓게
굴뚝으로 배출한 오염물질로
대기 중의 근로조건은 숨을
쉴 수 없을 만큼 악화,
구름 공장에서 작업하던 바람과
햇빛과 수증기가 일제히
파업을 단행하였다.

유례없는 대 가뭄.

지상의 초목들은 무참하게 시들어 간다.

전력 공급과 수도가 끊긴 이 한 여름 밤 서울의
찜통더위.

On Strike

By reason of the pollutants
pouring black from chimneys
the atmosphere's working conditions
had grown so bad they could not even breathe,
so the wind and sunlight and water vapor
that used to work in the cloud factory, with one accord
have agreed to go on strike.

An unprecendented total drought.

The earth's plants are withering pitifully.

This sweltering heat
tonight in midsummer Seoul, with electricity and water cut off.

화산 (2)

어느 공장에서 만든 제품들일까.
아름다운 꽃,
싱싱한 나무,
활기찬 짐승,
아아, 생각하는 인간도 있다.
밤낮 쉬지 않고
검은 연기를 내뿜는 저 거대하고 우람한
산정의 굴뚝을 보아라.
어느 용광로에 틈이 갔나.
수시로 불쑥 토해내는 뜨거운 마그마,
번쩍
전기 용접에서 튀는 번갯불,
간단없이 선반의 압착기가 두드리는
우레 소리,
그러나 아직 공급물량이 부족한 물품도
적지는 않다.

---중동의 사랑,
---한반도의 화해,
---미국의 희생,
---유럽의 양심,
---아프리카의 나눔,
---남미의 상생,

지구는 우주의 거대한 대장간, 그러나
지금은 지배인을 갈아야 할 때가
지나지 않았을까.
예수 혹은 석가
아니면 공자?

Volcano (2)

What factory were these produced in?
Beautiful flowers,
fresh green trees,
lively animals,
ah yes, and thinking humans too.
Consider that enormous, impressive mountaintop chimney
ceaselessly spouting black smoke.
Has some blast furnace developed a crack?
The burning hot magma constantly being ejected,
the lightning flashing like sparks from an electric welder,
the ceaseless throbbing thunder of compressors and lathes.
Yet there are plenty of things still
in short supply.

--- Love in the Middle East,
--- Reconciliation in the Korean peninsula,
--- Self-sacrifice in the United States,
--- Conscience in Europe,
--- Sharing in Africa,
--- Harmony in South America,

This world's the universe's great forge, but now
surely it's more than time
for a change of managers?
What about Jesus or the Buddha,
or perhaps Confucius?

그린벨트

어느새 자연은
전쟁터가 되었다,
격리된 수용소의 난민 일족이
굶주림에 지쳐 월경하다가
탕 탕
적탄에 맞아 쓰러진다.

숲속을 뛰쳐나와
잘 정리된 농지의 밭고랑에서
피 흘리며 나뒹구는 한 떼의
멧돼지.

자연과 대치하는 전선(戰線), 그리고
파아랗게 떨고 있는 대지.

Green Belt

At some point, nature
turned into a battle-field.
Refugee families from isolated camps,
weary with hunger, cross the border, then
bang, bang,
struck by enemy fire they fall.

Having come dashing out from the woods,
at the edge of well-tended farmland
a group of wild boars
lies scattered, bleeding.

The frontline confronting nature, and the earth
trembling, green.

동맥경화(動脈硬化)

단 몇 시간의
게릴라성 집중호우로 터져버린 뚝,
노오랗게 잘 익어가던 무논의 벼들이
한 순간
무섭게 들이닥친 급류에 휩쓸려
모조리 쓰러져 버렸다.
긴급복구,
앰뷸런스가 달려오고
차가운 침상의
의식을 잃어버린 심장에
메스를 든 의사들의 손놀림이 심각하다.
막힌 혈관을 찾아라.
관상동맥을 이어라.

야금야금 숲을 베고 능선을 뭉개버린 산지에서
흘러든 토사,
그 침전물로 막혀버린 무논의 수로(水路).

42

Hardening of the Arteries

The embankment yielded after a deluge
lasting just a few hours,
so the well-ripened yellow rice stalks in the paddies
all collapsed,
crushed by the torrent that came pouring in
abruptly.
Emergency repairs!
An ambulance comes speeding
and scalpel-wielding surgeons display their skill
on the unconscious heart
lying on the chill bed:
Find the blocked vein.
Join up the coronary arteries.

The earth and sand washed down
from the ridges that crumbled once the trees were cut down
had silted up the ditches serving the paddies.

인공 수분(受粉)

살충제, 제초제, 비료를 먹고 이 만큼
잘 자랐나?
어디를 보아도 튼실하고 멋진 몸매.

철만난 과원의 복숭아꽃 활짝 만개,
몸을 열었다.
그러나 아무리 꽃가루를 날려 보내도
정작 날아들지 않은 벌, 나비, 풍뎅이.

성희롱인가,
애꿎은 봄바람만 꽃잎을 살살 간질일 뿐.

과교육(過敎育)을 견지디 못해 가출한 양갓집
소녀 하나,
거리 부랑자의 손에 잡혀 그만
순결을 잃고 말았다.

Artificial Pollination

Fed with pesticide, herbicide, fertilizer, how well
they've all grown!
On all sides, sturdy, splendid growth.

In the orchard, the peach blossom is at its height,
all wide open.
But no matter how much pollen they send drifting,
no bees, butterflies, beetles come flying.

Is it sexual harassment?
The innocent spring breeze merely tickles the petals lightly.

One girl
from a respectable family, bored with studies, left home,
went walking hand in hand with a streetside loafer,
finally lost her virginity.

탁란(托卵)

양지바른 벌판
아늑한 둔덕에 쪼그리고 앉아
산은 오늘도
무덤들 몇 개를 품고 있다.
밖엔 겨울바람 매섭지만
포근하게 깃털로 감싼 가슴의 온기는
항상 따스하다.
언제 껍질을 깨고 나올까
그 알들……
산은 지상에 내려앉은
우주의 새,
품은 알 아직 부화할 기미가 없어
오늘도 날기를 포기한다.

Eggs in Another Nest

Sitting squat on cozy knolls
in sunny plains
the hills today
once more embrace a few graves.
Although outside the winter wind may be harsh,
their breasts, snugly wrapped in down,
are always warm.
When will the shells break and hatch?
Those eggs . . .
The hill is a cosmic bird
that has landed here on earth.
No sign yet that the eggs she is brooding are about to hatch,
so again today she renounces flight.

단풍

늦가을
계곡의 오색찬란하게 물든 단풍은
첫날밤
홀로 신랑을 맞이하는 신부의
고운 자태 같아라.

칠보단장에 원삼 족두리
연지 곤지 화사한 그
아미(蛾眉).

나무는
황홀한 밤의 아픔을 위하여
수줍게 옷 벗을 준비를 한다.

다시 올 봄이여.

Autumn Leaves

Late autumn.
The multi-colored foliage in the mountain valleys
recalls the lovely image
of a bride welcoming her husband
on the first night.

Beautiful slender eyebrows
over a bride's rouged cheeks,
bridal crown and gown adorned with the seven jewels.

The trees
are bashfully preparing to undress
for the pain of the blissful night.

Spring will come again.

춘설(春雪) (1)

운동회 전야(前夜)
잘 정비된 초등학교 운동장은
텅 비었지만 산뜻했다.
정문에서 교사까지
황토로 곱게 다져진 굳은 땅위에
하얗게 뿌려진 그 정갈한 횟가루.

내일의 축제로 가슴 설레는……

Spring Snow (1)

The night before the sports match
the well-maintained primary school yard
was quite empty but crisp.
From the front gate to the main building
on the clay of the firm, well-trodden path
that layer of graceful white powder sprinkled,
heart aflutter for tomorrow's festival . . .

춘설(春雪) (2)

초벌 그림은 아무래도
안되겠다.
다시 하얗게 지워버린 그 화판.

뒤척이다 늦 새벽 다시 꿈꾸는
백일몽!

Spring Snow (2)

The rough sketch somehow
won't do—
the drawing board erased, white again.

After tossing and turning, late dawn, dreaming again,
a daydream!

내 시의 사전에는 '증오'라는 말이 없다.

내 눈이 더 이상
전장의 살육을 보지 않게 하여라.
내 귀가 더 이상
산 자의 통곡을 듣지 않게 하여라.
내 코가 더 이상
대지의 피 냄새를 맡지 않게 하여라.
이 세상의 쇠붙이는 오직
옥토에 생명을 키우는 삽과 쟁기만을
만들지니
모든 총포와 창검과 그리고 철갑을 거두어
20세기의 비극 저
우리의 휴전선에
거대한 용광로를 하나 세우자.
미움과 원한과 저주와 분노를 녹여
아아, 한 가지 오직 화해만을 일구어낼
사랑의 용광로,
높은 장벽, 철조망, 쇠창살을 허문 바로 그 동산에
우리는 다만 꽃과 나무와 작물만을 심을 지니
이제 내 눈이 더 이상
전장의 살육을 보지 않게 하여라.
내 시의 사전에는
'증오' 라는 말이 없다.

The Word "Hatred" Does Not Figure in My Poetry's Dictionary

Keep my eyes from ever again seeing
battlefield's slaughter.
Keep my ears from ever again hearing
the wailing of the living.
Keep my nose from ever again smelling
the earth's stench of blood.
Since the world's iron would only serve
to make
spades and plows to raise life from fertile ground,
after gathering in all the guns and swords and armor
let's build a huge blast furnace
on our Armistice Line,
the twentieth century's tragedy,
a furnace of love
to melt down hatred and resentment and curses and anger
and produce, ah, nothing but reconciliation.
Tearing down high walls, barbed-wire fences, iron gratings,
on those hills we would plant nothing but flowers and trees and crops,
so keep my eyes from ever again seeing
battlefield's slaughter.
The word "hatred" does not figure
in my poetry's dictionary.

타종(打鐘)

낮고 깊은 신음소리,
날카로운 저 비명소리,
흉악범에게 가해지는 형벌의 나날인가.
발가벗겨 온 생을 허공에 매달린 채
종은 무시로
채찍에 맞아 울부짖는다.
누 만년 총칼로
창과 방패로, 탱크와 군함으로, 폭탄으로
평화를 짓밟고
수억 인류를 살상한 그
씻을 수 없는 죄.
그 쇠붙이 하나를 희생양으로 붙잡아 하늘에 고하고
단죄하나니
평화의 날을 기약하며
종신에 태형을 가하는 그
타종소리.

A Bell Being Rung

Low, deep groans,
piercing shrieks,
are they daily punishments of crime?
Hanging in the air, the bell
struck occasionally by whips
laments lives stripped naked.
For endless troubled ages, guns and swords,
spears and shields, tanks and warships, bombs were used
to trample down peace,
kill and maim countless victims,
an unforgivable crime,
and so one piece of iron was caught, reported to heaven,
found guilty,
and now, promising days of peace,
enduring a life sentence of flogging,
a bell is being rung.

이데올로기 (2)

야반도주인지 강제 이주인지 아무도 몰라.
주인이 떠난 지는 십 여 년이 넘었지만
대문은 아직 굳게
잠겨 있다.
이미 녹슨 지 오랜 자물쇠.
부숴야 열릴 문.
그 문틈으로 엿보는 집안은 폐허다.
가라앉은 지붕, 부서진 기둥, 나뒹구는 서까래,
개망초, 민들레,
정원의 무성한 잡초.
필시 그가 심었을
넝쿨장미 하나 월담해 밖으로 쫑긋
귀를 내밀어
내 그 꽃에게 행방을 묻노니
주인은 어디 가셨나?

아직 이름만 남아
바람이 불 때마다 아슬아슬 허공에 흔들리는
폐가(廢家)의 그 녹슨
문패.

Ideology (2)

Midnight flit or forced to relocate? Nobody knows but
it's more than ten years
since the owner left home,
yet the gate is still
firmly locked.
To open the gate you would have to smash
the long since rusted padlock.
The house glimpsed through the cracks is a wreck.
Roof fallen in, pillars broken, rafters scattered,
fleabane, dandelions,
the yard overgrown with weeds.
One rambler rose he must surely have planted
peeps out over the wall,
so I, pricking up my ears,
ask the flowers his whereabouts:
Where's the owner gone?

His name alone remains
on the deserted house's
rusty name-plate
that shakes dangerously whenever the wind blows.

이념

스스로 움직여 흐르지 않고
한 곳에 멈춰 고여 있는 것은 어차피
썩기 아니면 얼기다.
지하의 수맥 또한 그렇지 아니한가.
동토의 저 물상으로 굳어버린 나무와
수렁에서 썩어가는 풀을 보라.
나무가 혹은 풀이 간단없이
바람에 나부끼며 흔들려야 하는 이유를
알 것이다.
누가 그렇게 말했던가.
의식은 지하에 흐르는 물과 같아
투명하다고……
물은 토양의 정신, 항상
감성의 전율로 어디론가 흘러가야 할지니
고여 있는 그것을 우리는 일컬어
'이념'이라 한다.

Concept

Whatever does not move freely and flow
but stays put, stagnant in one place,
either rots or freezes, anyway.
Surely the same holds true of underground streams?
Only consider a tree made a rigid object in frozen ground
and plants rotting in a swamp.
You will see there
the reason why trees and plants ceaselessly
have to flutter and shake in the wind.
Who was it said
consciousness is like water flowing underground,
transparent . . . ?
Water, soil's spirit, always
has to be flowing with a shudder of sensitivity.
Once it stagnates, we call it
"concept."

자판기

무슨 죄를 지었기에 이처럼
격리 수용되어 있어야 하는가.
자판기는
식품들의 감옥일지 모른다.
똑같은 수의를 입고 칸칸마다
갇혀 있는
깡통 1, 깡통2, 깡통 3……
순수 식재료를
화학 첨가물로 오염시킨 죄일지 몰라.
방부제로
정신을 서서히 변질시킨 죄일지도 몰라.
가련해 보여서일까.
투입구에 몇 개의 동전을 넣자
철컥 철문이 열리며
쏟아져 나오는 형집행 정지 가석방 죄수들.
번번이 속아
보석을 신청하는 인간들의 그 순진함이
어리석기만 하다.

A Vending Machine

Is it because it committed some crime
that it has to be housed apart like this?
The vending machine
seems to be a prison for food.
All wearing the same uniform,
confined to each shelf,
Can 1, Can 2, Can 3 . . .
It might be the crime of polluting pure foodstuffs
with chemical additives.
It might be the crime of slowly adulterating minds
with preservatives.
Is it because it looks miserable?
As soon as a few coins are put in the slot,
the iron gate clangs open and
out pour paroled convicts with suspended sentences.
Fooled every time,
the naiveté of people applying for bail
is just stupid.

동파(凍破)

얼어붙은 경기로 주가 급락,
주식에 전 재산을 걸었던 한 실업 가장이
가족과
동반자살을 시도했다.
거실에 낭자한 피.

오늘 우리 집은 모든 것이 마비다.
시베리아에서 불어 온 냉기류에
기온 급강하,

보일러가 멈추고, 식수가 끊기고,
하수도가 막히고
믿었던 수도관의 동파.
평소
따뜻하게 감싸주지 못했던……

Freezing and Bursting

The economy froze, share prices nosedived,
one unemployed breadwinner whose whole savings were in
shares
committed suicide
along with his whole family.
Blood all over the sitting room.

Today our whole house is parlayzed.
With cold air blowing from Siberia
temperatures have nosedived.

The boiler's stopped, drinking water's cut off,
the drains are blocked,
the water main we relied on has frozen and burst.
Those I could usually
not protect or keep warm . . .

늦가을

현관 문기둥을 타고 올라
처마에서 지붕으로, 지붕에서 용마루로
쭉쭉 뻗어가던 넝쿨이
어젯밤 된 서리를 맞아 쭉정이만 남았다.
여름내 무성했던 초록 잎새들이 어느새 갈잎져,
남발된 부도수표처럼
마당에 수북이 쌓여 있다.
바람에 이리저리 날린다.
그래도 구둣발에 밟히지 않으려는 듯
미처 거두지 못한 조롱박 하나가
익지도 못한 채 시들어
처마 끝 파아란 하늘에 대롱대롱
매달려 있다.

어제까지 승승장구,
최고로 치솟던 주가(株價)가 그만
경기 한파로
하룻밤 새 갑자기 폭락한 뒤
그 중년 실업가는 자신의 사무실 천정에 그만
목을 맸다.

Late Autumn

Stricken by last night's frost,
nothing but a withered stalk remained of the creeper
that had wound its way up a pillar of the porch,
then spread from eaves to roof, from roof to roof-ridge.
The green leaves that flourished all summer long abruptly
withered
and now lie piled in the yard
like a mound of bad checks.
They fly hither and thither in the wind.
Still, reluctant to trample them underfoot,
a single gourd I had been unable to pick,
that wilted before it had ripened,
is still dangling from the edge of the eaves.

Stock prices, which until yesterday
had been constantly climbing ever higher,
suddenly fell overnight
as the economy froze,
so a middle-aged businessman hanged himself
from his office ceiling.

농성(籠城)

매장엔 찬바람만 분다.
체감 경기는 이미 빙점(氷點) 이하
부도 직전의 회사는 문을 닫았다.
일시에
거리로 내몰린 실직 노동자들은 바람 따라
뿔뿔이 흩어졌는데
대량 해고에 항의하며 아슬아슬
타워 크레인 첨탑 끝에 앉아 단식 농성에 돌입한
그 사원 하나.

떨어지길 거부한 채
벼랑의 나뭇가지 끝에 홀로 매달려
위태위태
겨울바람에 흔들리고 있는 저 외로운 갈잎
하나.

Sit-in

A cold wind is blowing through the store.
With the economic forecast already below freezing,
the company closed down on the verge of bankruptcy.
At the same time,
the workers who lost their jobs, driven onto the streets,
have scattered with the wind.
But one employee,
protesting against the mass layoffs,
is staging a hunger strike poised at the tip of a tower crane.

Refusing to fall,
hanging all alone at the tip of a lofty branch,
perilously
swaying in the winter wind, one lonely, withered
leaf.

권력

산책 길 풀 섶에서
불쑥 뛰쳐나온 한 마리 뱀,
놀라 한 발짝 물러서서 다시 들여다보니
썩은 새끼줄이다.
객쩍은 마음에 절로 웃음이 난다.
한 때는 누군가 목을 맸을 혹은
옴짝 달싹 못하도록 사지를 결박했을
그 새끼줄.
살아서 공포의 대상이었던 그가
이제는 죽어 조롱감이다.
줄을 대고, 줄을 세워, 줄로서 줄줄이 줄을 묶어
뱀처럼 교활하게
한 세상 또아리를 틀었던 그
권력이
실은 한 토막 썩은 새끼줄이었던가.
무엇이든 묶어 방치된 줄은
언제인가 한번은 녹슬거나 썩는 법.
나 오늘 산책길에서
부패도 아름다울 수 있음을
처연히 깨우친다.

Power

Suddenly, from the grassy verge of the path,
a snake emerges.
Startled, I take a step backwards and look again.
It's a scrap of rotten rope.
Laughter erupts in my idle heart.
That rope,
which someone once hanged himself with,
or was bound by, hand and foot, so he could not move,
alive, was a source of dread,
but now, dead, it inspires ridicule.
Pulling strings, roping in, tying up in knots,
cunningly coiled like a snake
all its life long,
was that power
really nothing but a scrap of rotten rope?
A rope thrown away after being used to tie something
is bound to rust or rot one day.
Today, taking this path,
sadly I recognize
that rotting also has its beauty.

좌냐 우냐

사원 공채 면접 보러가는 날,
회사 찾기 난망이다.
한참 길을 찾다보면 우회로(迂廻路),
다시 걷다 보면 또
구도로(舊道路),
좌냐, 우냐, 마주치는 교차로의 횡단보도에
어리둥절 멈춰 서서
잠시 고개를 돌려보는데
안하무인
휘익
고속으로 질주하는 작업차량에 치어
아차
죽을 번 하였다.
군용 트럭이 아니길 다행.

어딘들 바다에 가 닿지 않으랴.
굽이굽이 몇 천리 뻗어 있는 길,
강물도 물길 따라 흐른다지만
좌냐, 우냐,
그 어디에도 교차로가 없는 강,
교통사고 없는 강.

Right or Left?

The day of the job interview,
finding the office is quite memorable.
Trying to find the way, a detour,
walking on
the old road again,
is it right or left? Pausing bewildered
at an intersection crosswalk,
briefly looking to one side,
disdainful,
Screech!
struck by a speeding van,
Wow!
I nearly died.
Lucky it wan't an army truck.

Suppose I head for the sea?
Winding on for mile after mile,
a river also flows following its course.
But a river has no intersections,
no right or left?
A river has no traffic accidents.

비정규직

깨져서 모난
파편이 되지도 못한다.
유리병이나 사기그릇과는 다른
일회용 종이컵.
근처에 자판기가 있는 것일까,
보도 이곳저곳 함부로 버려져 발길에
채이고 있다.
한 순간
미각(味覺)을 자극하던 그 씁쓸하고도
달콤한 관능,
커피 한 모금 훌쩍 빨아 마시고 내 팽개친
그 새하얀 순정,
밟혀 구겨지지 않는 것은
종이컵이 아니다.
깨지면 칼날이 되는
유리병과는 다르다. 그 일회용 종이컵,
대량해고로
일시에 거리거리 내 몰린 비정규직
노동자들.

Temporary Workers

It can never break
into sharp-angled debris,
unlike a glass bottle or china bowl—
a disposable paper cup.
There must be a vending machine nearby,
it's been thrown down on the sidewalk
and is being kicked about by passing feet.
The bitter-sweet physicality that once
briefly
stimulated a palate,
the pure, white love
flung down after sucking in a mouthful of coffee,
not trampled and crumpled,
is no paper cup.
It's unlike a glass bottle that turns into knife blades
once it's broken. That disposable paper cup
is temporary workers
driven out onto the streets
by mass layoffs.

아이. 엠. 에프(IMF)

늦여름
남태평양에서 형성된 고기압이 돌연
태풍을 몰고 북상하더니
쓰나미를 동반
단숨에 한반도 해안을 강타했다.
잘 익어가던 과원의 능금들이
우두둑 떨어져
진흙구덩이에 나뒹군다.

가을로 가는 막차는 이미 떠났는데
기약 없이 기다리다가
맨바닥에 아무렇게나 쓰러져 잠든
여름역 대합실의 실직
노숙자들.

IMF

Late summer,
a high pressure system in the South Pacific abruptly
turned northward, bringing a typhoon with it
and a tidal surge,
that smashed aginst the Korean coast.
The apples that had been ripening so well in the orchards
came showering down
and lay scattered in the mud.

The last train for winter has left already
but, still hanging around just in case,
these unemployed down-and-outs
lie sprawled sleeping on the bare floor
of the summer station's waiting room.

암초

입 안에 드는 것은 때로 육신을
병들게 하지만
귀로 드는 것은 마음에 상처를 낸다.
공해물질에 오염된 식품을 먹고
걸린 암, 그러나
한 순간의 폭언(暴言)이 격발시킨 그
광적(狂的) 원한,
육신의 병은 자신을 죽게 만들지만
마음의 병은 타인을 해친다.
천길 물속은 알아도
한길 마음속은 모른다 하나
언뜻 잔잔해 보이는 수면 아래서 몰래
밀물과 썰물로 칼을 갈고 있는
그 바다 속 암초.

A Rock

What enters through the mouth sometimes
makes the body sick
but what enters through the ear wounds the heart.
There are cancers inflicted
by eating polluted food, but
there's the intense resentment
provoked by a moment's verbal violence.
If the body is sick in the end you may die,
but when the heart is sick others are harmed.
They say you may know what's in water a thousand fathoms
deep
yet know nothing of what's in a single fathom of heart,
so what about that rock beneath the sea,
its blade sharpened in secret by rising and ebbing tides
beneath a seemingly placid surface?

연(鳶)

위로 위로 오르고자 하는 것은 그 무엇이든
바람을 타야 한다.
그러나 새처럼, 벌처럼, 나비처럼 지상으로
돌아오길 원치 않는다면
항상
끈에 매달려 있어야 하는 것,
양력(揚力)과 인력(引力)이 주는 긴장과 화해,
그 끈을 끊고
위로 위로 바람을 타고 오른 것들의 행방을
나는 모른다.
다만 볼 수 있었던 것,
갈기갈기 찢겨져 마른 나뭇가지에 걸린
연, 혹은 지상에 나뒹구는 풍선 파편들,
확실한 정체는 모르지만
이름들은 많았다.
마파람, 샛파람, 하늬 바람, 된 바람, 회오리, 용오름……

이름이 많은 것들을 믿지 마라.
바람난 남자와 바람난 여자가 바람을 타고
아슬 아슬
허공에 짓던 집의 실체를 나 오늘
추락한 연에서 본다.

A Kite

Anything that longs to rise upward, upward,
must ride the wind.
But if like birds, like bees, like butterflies
they do not want to return to earth,
always
having to be hanging on a string,
reconciling the tension between lift and gravity,
I know nothing
of the whereabouts of those things that,
snapping the string, have ridden the wind upward, upward.
Only things that could still be seen,
a kite hanging tattered among dry branches
or scraps of a baloon scattered on the ground,
I am unsure of their precise identity
but they had many names.
South wind, east wind, west wind, howling gale, tornado,
whirlwind . . .

Never trust things with multiple names.
A flirtatious man and a flighty lady, riding the wind
thrillingly,
building a house in the air, that is really what I see today
in a fallen kite.

손목시계

근대에 들어
신(神)이 죽었다고 떠벌리는 인간들에게 신은
신성 모독의 벌로
손목에 시간의 수갑을 채웠다.
인간들이
성범죄자의 발목에
전자 팔찌를 채우는 것처럼……

A Wristwatch

As they entered modernity
people boasted that God was dead, so God
fastened times manacle round their wrists
in punishment for their blasphemy.
Just as people fix an electronic bracelet
round the ankles of sex offenders . . .

갯바위

찰진 흙같이
숲과 꽃밭을 일굴 수는 없겠으나
다른 바위가 그런 것처럼 스스로 금가
그 틈새로
난초꽃 한 그루도 피울 수 없다는 것이냐.
마른 이끼 한 뿌리도 키울 수 없다는 것이냐.
그 불붙은 응어리를 한으로 삭혀
가슴 깊이 굳혀버린 저
용암의 숯덩이.
이리저리
강물 따라 구만리 굴러온 바위 하나,
제 운명과 맞서 차라리 죽음을
선택했다.
벼랑 끝에서
까마득히 바다로 투신해
수면 위로 머리를 내민 채 허우적거리는
갯바위 하나.

Seaside Rock

Viscous mud
may never grow into forests or flowerbeds,
but how could any other rock, like that, not crack
then in that crevice
allow one orchid to bloom?
Not allow one dry ivy root to grow?
Such burning resentment fermented, grew bitter,
hardened deep in the heart
of a lump of lava.
Rolled hither and thither
mile after mile in a river's flow, one chunk of rock
resisted its fate, prefered
to die.
From the top of a cliff
it hurled itself down into the sea,
and flounders there, its head above water,
one seaside rock.

해머

홀로 있다는 것은
있지 않다는 것이다. 아니
없다는 것이다.
언덕에 쳐 박힌 바위,
홀로 길가에 버려진 돌멩이,
어디 그들을 살아 있다 하겠는가.
생명은 항상 누군가와 만나서
부딪히고, 깨지고, 합치고, 나뉘고, 열 받아야
생명이다.
한 자리만을 지키는 나무나 꽃도 기실
바람에 흔들리고 벌이 핥아
살아 있는 것.
아무 만남 없이 홀로 시간을 죽이는 인간보다는
부딪히는 두 개의 돌멩이가 더 의미 있나니
해머가 내리치는 정(釘)에 맞아
쩡
한 순간 반동하는 바위의 강한
힘,
파아랗게 번쩍이는 그
불꽃을 보라.

Hammer

Whatever claims to exist alone
cannot be said to exist. Or rather,
does not exist.
A rock stuck high on a hill,
a stone abandoned by the roadside—
how can such things be said to be alive?
Being alive always means meeting some other,
being struck, broken, united, divided, being upset,
that's what life is.
Trees and flowers may be fixed to one spot, but in fact
it's when they're shaken by the wind, sucked by bees
that they come alive.
Rather than someone all alone, meeting nobody, killing time,
two pebbles colliding have more meaning.
When a hammer drops and strikes a nail,
Bang,
the power of a rock briefly recoiling,
sparkling red,
just see that flame.

풍선

축제 때마다
일제히 하늘로 날리는
풍선.
어떤 것은 나뭇가지에,
어떤 것은 전신주에 걸려 안타깝지만
시야에서 멀리 사라졌다고 하여 어찌
하늘에 닿았다 하겠는가.
필경 낮은 기압에 터지고 뜨거운 햇살에 타서
몇 조각 시신으로 지상에 추락할 지니
태양은 항상
절대의 높이에서 군림해야 할 존재,
그 누구든 결코
근접을 허락지 않는다.

그러므로 축제 때 풍선을 날리는 까닭은
들뜬 마음을 가라앉혀 스스로
자신의 분수를 알라는 뜻일지니
진실은
보이지 않는다 해서 결코 사라지는 법이
아니다.

Balloons

Every time there's a festival,
all those baloons
rising together into the sky.
Some, alas, end up caught in tree branches,
some hanging on utility poles,
but even if some vanish from sight in the distance
that does not mean they touch the sky.
Either they burst in the rarefied air or burn up in the sun's heat
and fall to earth as a few scraps of corpse.
For the sun, always,
is a being who reigns absolute in height
and none may approach him.

Therefore, balloons are released at festivals
to calm excited hearts
and remind them of their proper place,
for although the truth
cannot be seen, that does not mean
it disappears.

아하!

아직 채 겨울은 가지 않았는데
눈밭에서
바싹 마른 마가목 꽃대의 막
트는 눈이
눈을 뜨고 새초롬히 바라다보는
유리 하늘.

동안거(冬安居) 막바지에 이른 수좌(首座)의
정결한 이마 아래서 빛나는 푸른
눈빛 같다.

아하!
깨달음은 듣는 것이 아니라
보는 것,
반짝
한 세상이 그의 눈 안에 드는 것.

Aha!

Winter was not yet past
but in the snow
the shifting snow
on the dry flower stalks of the rowan trees
opens its eyes, gazes up at the chilly seeming
glassy sky.

It is like the azure gaze shining
beneath the pure brow
of a meditating monk near the end of the winter session.

Aha!
Enlightenment is not a matter of hearing
but of seeing,
in a flash
a whole lifetime entering his eyes.

파도는

간단없이 밀려드는 파도는
해안에 부딪혀 스러짐이 좋은 것이다.
아무 미련 없이
산산히 무너져 제자리로 돌아가는
최후가 좋은 것이다.
파도는
해안에 부딪혀 흰 포말로 돌아감이 좋은 것이다.
그를 위해 소중히 지켜온
자신의 지닌 모두 것들을 후회 없이 갖다 바치는
그 최선이 좋은 것이다.
파도는
해안에 부딪혀 고고하게 부르짖는 외침이 좋은 것이다.
오랜 세월 가슴에 품었던 한마디 말을
확실히 고백할 수 있는 그 결단의 순간이 좋은 것이다.
아, 간단없이 밀려드는 파도는
거친 대양을 넘어서, 사나운 해협을 넘어서
드디어
해안에 도달하는 그 행적이 좋은 것이다.
스러져 수평으로 돌아가는
그 한 생이 좋은 것이다.

Waves

The way the waves come surging ceaselessly,
strike the shore then collapse, is good.
The final stage,
as they collapse in spray and return to their place
without any hesitation, is good.
The way the waves, after breaking on the shore,
return home as foam is good.
Their devotion,
offering up without regret all they possess,
all that they had kept in store for that, is good.
The cry
the aloof waves make as they break on the shore is good.
That moment of decision, when they are able at last to express
directly the word they had long been storing in their hearts, is good.
Ah, the trail of those ceaselessly surging waves
that finally,
after passing over the rough ocean, the wild straights,
break on the shore, is good.
That life, collapsing
and returning back toward the horizon, is good,

가을 단풍

불은
산소 없이
연료만으로는 안 된다.
불씨를 살려내기 위해서는 누구나 조심스레
솔솔 입김을 불어야 한다.
하나, 둘……
봄바람에 흔들리며 깨어나는 꽃들,
그 첫사랑.

그러나 바람난 욕정은 쉽게
불길을 잡을 수 없다.
늦여름의 태풍을 견디지 못하고
활활 타서 한껏 재가 되어버린
가을 단풍을 보아라.

Autumn Maples

A fire
is not possible with fuel alone
and no oxygen.
In order to give life to a spark, everyone
must carefully blow on it.
One, two . . .
Flowers waking as a spring breeze shakes them,
that first love.

But promiscuous desire cannot
so easily contain the flame.
Only look at the autumn maples,
unable to endure late summer typhoons
they blazed fiercely and were all reduced to ashes.

낙하

꽃잎들은 하늘 하늘 하늘로 날아가지만
열매들은
흔쾌히 지상으로 뛰어내린다.

이상은 멀리 지평선 넘어 있어도
현실은 발 아래
중력을 무시할 수 없는 법.

바람이 분다.
… 털석 …
생명의 중심을 향해
망설이지 않고 몸을 던지는 그
용기,

우주에 잔잔히 파문이 인다.

이 세상에는 그 무엇도
결별 없이 깨어나는 삶이란 없다.
수직과 수평이 교차하는 가지 끝에서
오늘도
조용히 바람에 흔들리고 있는
나무.

The Fall

Petals fluttering fluttering go flying skyward
but fruit
gladly leap down to the ground.

Though ideals may lie far beyond the horizon,
the reality beneath our feet
cannot ignore gravity.

The wind blows.
... *Plop* ...
Throwing itself unhesitatingly
toward life's center—
such courage.

Ripples gently run through the cosmos.

In this world, everything,
no life awakes without separation.
At the end of branches intersecting, vertical and horizontal,
today as ever
quietly shaking in the wind,
a tree.

어떤 기도

기도하는 갈매기를 보았는가.
허공을 선회하던 갈매기 한 떼가
돌연
뭍으로 내리더니
해안 사구에 정연히 자리를 잡고
해를 바래 조용히 명상에 든다.
수평선 너머 한 방향을 일제히 응시하는 그
눈빛들이 경건하다.
머리에는 한결같이 흰 깃의 히잡을 썼다.
모스크 광장에 도열해서
메카를 향해 무릎을 꿇고 경배하는
무슬림들 같다.
잠시 전
고깃배에서 활어를 약탈하고,
어시장에서 생선 찌꺼기를 훔쳐 먹고,
날쌔게 잠수해서 어린 물고기를 살육하던
그 모습이 아니다.
갈매기도
험난한 바다에선 삶이 고해임을 아는 까닭에
이처럼 신에게
고백할 줄을 아는 것이다.

A Kind of Prayer

Did you ever see a praying seagull?
A flock of gulls after wheeling through the air
abruptly
drops down to the beach.
Settling in order on the dunes by the shore,
gazing sunward, they quietly start to meditate.
The gaze of each and all is devoutly fixed in one direction
on something that lies beyond the horizon.
Over their heads, as ever, they all wear a white hijab.
They are like Muslims lined up in a mosque courtyard,
on their knees in worship
facing toward Mecca.
They give no sign of how
just before
they had been plundering live fish from fishing boats,
gobbling up offal stolen from the fish market,
plunging quickly under water to slaughter baby fish.
Because they know they have to live in the bitter sea,
they likewise know
how to confess their sins to God.

하수아비

구획 정리가 잘된 농지는
식물들의 아파트 단지인지도 몰라.
도시 셀러리맨 같은 작물들의
출퇴근이 정확하다.
자연의 시간은 일 년이 하루다.
지금 시각은 오후 6시,
가을의 시작.
거리는
일제히 퇴근길을 서두르는 인파들로
북적거린다.
한 밤은 겨울,
인적 끊긴 단지 내엔 몇몇 경비원들만
무료하게
적막한 집들을 지키고 있다.
허수아비, 허수아비,
봄을 기다리며
먼 산맥을 말없이 응시하고 서 있는
겨울 들녘의 저 허수아비.

Scarecrows

Well-laid-out farmlands do not realize
that they are apartment complexes for plants.
The commuting hours of crops
are precise like city office workers'.
In Nature's time-scheme a year is a single day.
Now it's six in the evening,
the beginning of autumn.
The streets
are all bustling with crowds
hastening homeward.
Midnight is winter,
and in the deserted subdivisions just a few night guards
are keeping watch over the silent houses.
Scarecrow, scarecrow,
waiting for springtime,
gazing in silence at the distant mountains,
in the winter fields, those scarecrows.

울음

산다는 것은 스스로
울 줄을 안다는 것이다.
누군가를 울릴 수 있다는 것이다.
갖 태어나
탯줄을 목에 감고 우는 아기,
빈 나무 끝에 홀로 앉아
먼 하늘을 향해 우짖는 새,
모두 처마 끝에 매달린 풍경같이
울고
또 울린다.
삶의 순간은 항상 만남과 헤어짐의
연속임으로……
바람이 우는 것이냐. 전깃줄이 우는 것이냐.
오늘도 나는 빈 들녘에 홀로 서서
겨울바람에 울고 있는 전신주를 보았다.
그들은 절실한 것이다.
물건도 자신의 운명이 줄에 걸릴 때는
울 줄을 아는 것이다.

Weeping

Being alive is a matter of
knowing how to cry,
of knowing how to make an other cry.
A newborn babe
crying with the cord wound round its neck,
perched alone at the tip of a branch,
a bird crying to the distant sky,
all, like wind chimes ringing suspended from eaves,
cry
and move to tears.
Since every lifetime is always a series
of meetings and partings . . .
Is it the wind that's crying, or is it the power lines?
Today, standing alone out in the empty fields
I saw utility poles crying in the winter wind.
They are so intense.
Objects, too, when their fate is on the line
know how to cry.

첫날 밤

   ---안성에 우거할 집 한 채를 짓고

거푸집을 뜯어내자
신축 건물 하나 눈부시게 속살을 드러낸다.
허물 벗은 매미처럼 그 모습
산뜻하다.
단아한 선의 콩크릿 외벽,
사슴의 푸른 눈망울 같은 유리창,
대리석 이마의 둥근 베란다, 그리고
그 속눈섭 커틴,
온 방의 전등들을 일시에 켜본다.
드디어 입택이다.

드디어 첫날밤이다.
오랜 세월 몸을 가린 옷들을 벗어던지고
처음으로 보여주는 그대의 나신,
맨몸과 맨몸이 만나서 등불을 켜든
오늘은 축일.

The First Night

—After building a house to live in

Once the shuttering is removed
a new building dazzles as it reveals its bare skin.
Like a cicada newly emerging from its cocoon, it looks
so fresh.
The external walls with their graceful lines,
windows like a deer's green eyes,
the curved veranda with its marble brow, and
those eyelash curtains,
I turn on the lights in all the rooms.
In My Home at last.

At last, the first night.
I throw off the clothes that for so long veiled our bodies,
revealing for the first time your nudity,
bare body unites with bare body, and even without lanterns lit
today is a festival.

EARLIER POEMS

그릇

깨진 그릇은
칼날이 된다.

절제와 균형의 중심에서
빗나간 힘,
부서진 원은 모를 세우고
이성의 차가운
눈을 뜨게 한다.

맹목(盲目)의 사랑을 노리는
사금파리여,
지금 나는 맨발이다.
베어지기를 기다리는
살이다.
상처 깊숙히서 성숙하는 혼(魂)

깨진 그릇은
칼날이 된다.
무엇이나 깨진 것은
칼이 된다.

A Bowl

A broken bowl
becomes a blade.

When might goes astray
amidst moderation and balance,
broken circles
make a sharp edge
and force open reason's
ice-cold eyes.

Ah, potsherd aimed
at unseeing love,

I am barefoot now.
I am flesh
waiting to be slashed.
A soul maturing since the wound is deep.

A broken bowl
becomes a blade.
Any broken thing
becomes a blade.

음악

잎이 지면
겨울 나무들은 이내
악기가 된다.
하늘에 걸린 음표에 맞춰
바람의 손끝에서 우는
악기,

나무만은 아니다.
계곡의 물소리를 들어보아라.
얼음장 밑으로 공명하면서
바위에 부딪혀 흐르는 물도
음악이다.

윗가지에서는 고음이,
아랫가지에서는 저음이 울리는 나무는
현악기,
큰 바위에서는 강음이
작은 바위에서는 약음이 울리는 계곡은
관악기.

오늘처럼
천지에 흰 눈이 하얗게 내려
그리운 이의 모습이 지워진 날은
창가에 기대어 음악을
듣자.

감동은 눈으로 오기보다
귀로 오는 것,
겨울은 청각으로 떠오르는 무지개다.

Music

When their leaves have fallen
the winter trees
turn into musical instruments,
instruments
ringing out at the wind's fingertips,
following the notes hanging in the sky.

And not only trees.
Listen to the streams in the valleys.
Water bouncing off rocks as it flows
echoing under sheets of ice
is music too.

The tree where high notes ring from high branches,
low notes from low branches,
is a stringed instrument,
the valley where loud notes ring from big rocks,
quiet notes from small rocks,
is a wind instrument.

On a day like today
when snow has fallen white over the world,
the image of the one we yearn for effaced,
I want to listen to music
leaning here beside my window.

Emotions come through the ear
rather than the eye,
winter is a rainbow emerging through hearing.

눈물

물도 불로 타오를 수 있다는 것은
슬픔을 가져본 자만이
안다.
여름날
해 저무는 바닷가에서
수평선 너머 타오르는 노을을
보아라.
그는 무엇이 서러워
눈이 붉도록 울고 있는가.
뺨에 흐르는 눈물의 흔적처럼
갯벌에 엉기는 하이얀
소금기,
소금은 슬픔의 숯덩이다.
사랑이 불로 타오르는
빛이라면
슬픔은 물로 타오르는 빛,
눈동자에 잔잔히 타오르는 눈물이
어둠을
밝힌다.

Tears

Only one who has experienced sorrow
knows
that water can also burst into flames.
Only look at the crimson blaze
rising from the horizon on a summer's day
beside the sea at sunset.
It's as if it is so sad about something
that it has wept until its eyes are red.
White salt
crystallizing on the mud
like traces of tears on a cheek:
salt is the charcoal of love.
If we say that love is light
rising as fire,
sorrow is light rising as water,
and tears rising gently in the eyes
make the darkness bright.

신(神)의 하늘에도 어둠은 있다

내가 원고지의 빈칸에
ㄱ, ㄴ, ㄷ, ㄹ……
글자를 뿌리듯
신은 밤하늘에
별들을 뿌린다.
빈 공간은 왜 두려운 것일까,
절대의 허무를
빛으로 메꾸려는 저, 신의
공간,
그러나 나는 그것을
말씀으로 채우려 한다.
내가 원고지의 빈칸에
ㄱ, ㄴ, ㄷ, ㄹ…… 글자를 뿌릴 때
지상에 떨어지는 씨앗들은
꽃이 되고 풀이 되고 또
나무가 되지만
언제인가 그들 또한
빈 공간으로 되돌아간다.
나와 너의 먼 거리에서
유성의 불꽃으로 소멸하는
언어,
빛이 있으므로 신의 하늘에도
어둠은 있다.

There Is Darkness in God's Heaven Too

Just as I scatter letters one by one
a, b, c, d ...
on the empty lines of my page,
God scatters stars
in the evening sky.
Why should empty space be so frightening?
God's space up there,
eager to stop up with light
the void of the Absolute,
while I try to fill it
with words.
When I scatter letters one by one
a, b, c, d ... on the empty lines of my page
the seeds that fall to the ground
grow into flowers, and plants, and
trees but yet
sooner or later they all return
back into empty space.
Language
vanishing like the blaze of a shooting star
in the distances separating you and me,
and since there is light there is darkness
in God's heaven too.

적막(寂寞)

　'아' 하고 외치면 '아' 하고 돌아온다.
　'아' 다르고 '어' 다른데
　'아' 와 '어' 틀림없이 다르게 돌아오는 그
산울림,
누가 불렀을까,
산 벚나무엔 다시 산 벚꽃 피고
산 딸나무엔 다시 산 딸꽃 핀다.
미움과 사랑도 이와같아라.
눈물 부르면 눈물이,
웃음 부르면 웃음 오느니
저무는 봄 강가에 홀로 서서
어제는 너를 실려보내고 오늘은 또
나를 실려보낸다.
흐르는 물에
텅 빈 얼굴을 들여다보는
눈이 부시게 푸르른 봄날 오후의
그 적막.

Solitude

If I shout "ah!" an "ah!" comes back.
"Ah!" is one thing, "oh!" another,
and the echo in the hills
unfailingly sends them back differently.
On wild cherry trees wild cherry flowers blossom,
on wild plum trees wild plum flowers bloom:
I wonder who called them forth?
Love and hate are just the same.
If you call for tears, tears will come,
if you call for smiles, then smiles will come.
Standing by the river at sunset in springtime
yesterday sent you off and today in turn
sends me off.
This solitude
on a spring afternoon, the sky dazzlingly blue,
as I gaze at my quite empty face
reflected in the flowing water.

드라마

고인 물은 그림이 되지만
흐르는 물은
언어가 된다.

호수는 산을
바다는 하늘을 담은 수채화,
그 적막한 공간의
응시.

그러므로 흐르는 물은 말로
산과
하늘을 담고자 한다.
크고 작은 혹은
깊고 얕은 그의 음성,

꽃 덤불 지나면 속삭이고
면울 물 만나면 웅얼대고
바위에 부딪치면 고함 지르는
물은
아, 절벽이다.

격정의 순간에 파멸하는
주인공의 운명, 그
추락.
드라마는 떨어지는 물이다.

흐르는 물은 산문이 되지만
폭포의 떨어지는 물은
드라마가 된다.

Drama

Still water becomes a picture,
but flowing water
becomes language.

The lake is a water-color holding the hills,
the sea, the sky,
the stare
of those lonely spaces.

So now the flowing water tries to hold in words,
the hills
and the sky.
Its sound great or small,
deep or shallow,

Water
murmuring as it passes bushes in bloom,
babbling as it encounters shallows,
roaring as it breaks against rocks,
is ah . . . a cliff.

The fate of the protagonist
ruined by an hour of passion,
that fall!
The drama is falling water.

Flowing water becomes prose
but a waterfall's water
becomes a drama.

열매

세상의 열매들은 왜 모두
둥글어야 하는가.
가시나무도 향기로운 그의 탱자만은 둥글다.

땅으로 땅으로 파고드는 뿌리는
날카롭지만,
하늘로 하늘로 뻗어가는 가지는
뾰족하지만
스스로 익어 떨어질 줄 아는 열매는
모가 나지 않는다.

덥썩
한입에 물어 깨무는
탐스런 한 알의 능금
먹는 자의 이빨은 예리하지만
먹히는 능금은 부드럽다.

그대는 아는가,
모든 생성하는 존재는 둥글다는 것을
스스로 먹힐 줄 아는 열매는
모가 나지 않는다는 것을.

Fruit

I wonder why all the fruit in the world
have to be round.
On the spiny branches of the thorny orange
the scented fruit alone are round.
The roots delving down down into the ground
are sharp,
the branches stretching up up into the sky
are pointed,
but the fruit, quite able to ripen and drop for themselves,
show no signs of any angles.

A single crab-apple
that can be bitten and devoured in a single
munch:
The teeth of the eater may be sharp,
the crab-apple being eaten is soft.

Did you ever realize that
everything that is coming into being is round?
That fruit, knowing they are going to be eaten,
never develop angles?

원시 遠視

멀리 있는 것은
아름답다.
무지개나 별이나 벼랑에 피는 꽃이나
멀리 있는 것은
손에 닿을 수 없는 까닭에
아름답다.
사랑하는 사람아,
이별을 서러워하지 마라,
내 나이의 이별이란
헤어지는 일이 아니라 단지
멀어지는 일일 뿐이다.
네가 보낸 마지막 편지를 읽기 위해선
이제
돋보기가 필요한 나이,
늙는다는 것은
사랑하는 사람을 멀리 보낸다는
것이다.
머얼리서 바라다볼 줄을
안다는 것이다.

Farsightedness

Far-off things
are beautiful.
Rainbows, stars, or flowers blooming on cliffs,
far-off things,
are beautiful
because they can't be touched.
You who love me,
do not grieve over parting
for parting at my age is
not separation but merely
a simple matter of moving farther off.
The age at which I need glasses
now
in order to read your last letter,
growing old,
is something
that sends the one I love farther away.
It's a matter of knowing
how to see from far away.

낙과

하늘을 향해 쑥쑥 자라는 나무는
지상의 가장 높은 곳에
열매를 맺고자 하지만
그는 모른다.
그 자란 높이만큼
떨어지지 않으면 안된다는 것을,
그 자란 높이만큼
떨어지는 아픔도 크다는 것을,
아래로 아래로 추락하는 물만이
바다에 이르듯
나무는 더 이상 하늘에 닿을 수 없음을
깨달을 때, 비로소
절망을 배운다.
절망의 벼랑 끝에서
툭
떨어지는 눈물처럼
떨어지는
낙과.

Fruit Falls

The tree that grows up and up toward heaven
longs to bear fruit
in the highest place in the world
but it does not realize
that it is bound to fall down
as far as it has grown up,
that the pain that comes from falling
as far as it has grown up is great.
Just as only water that falls on and on downward
finally reaches the sea,
the day when it finally realizes that it
cannot get any closer to touching the sky,
a tree learns despair.
At the foot of the cliff of despair,
plop,
like falling tears
fruit
falls.